What Do They See When They See You Coming?

The Power Of Perception Over Reality

*How They
Perceive
You Is
Your
Business!*

Stephen M. Gower, CSP

Lectern Publishing
P. O. Box 1065, Toccoa, GA 30577

First edition, published 1993 by LECTERN PUBLISHING, P.O. Box 1065, Toccoa, GA 30577.
NinthPrinting, 2005.

Library of Congress Catalog Card No. 93-79279

ISBN 1-880150-01-8

Dedication

This book is dedicated to my grandmother, Weezie. For 103 years, Weezie blessed the North Georgia hills with a gentle directness, a subtle wit and a classic grace.

The strength of a giant emanated from her diminutive frame and, particularly during adolescence, I would find her company a welcome retreat.

When I saw Weezie coming, I always perceived her love.

Weezie, I love you still.

Acknowledgments

I have traditionally utilized this section as a vehicle for recognizing the support and encouragement of my family and friends. I have certainly appreciated their understanding during the writing of my books, particularly this one. I well recognize that cantankerous behavior often accompanies a small portion of creativity.

In this instance, I prefer that a significant part of the acknowledgment section be used to state my appreciation for the corporate and association managers with whom I have worked.

I constantly notice that some of my grandest tutors are my clients and their staffs. Accordingly, I acknowledge that my comprehension of the power of perception has been positively enhanced by the companies for whom I provide consultation and by the clients for whom I speak.

The mission of *What Do They See When They See You Coming?* is to encourage a journey into introspection, affirm the power of another's perception and present possible behavioral modifications.

Contents

The Trail And A Tale

An Introduction

What Do They See When They See You Coming? is an invitation into introspection. It encourages the manager or leader to ask a question that leads to a second opinion – the opinion of the employee, the follower, the customer, the student, the family member. This second opinion, coupled with his own opinion, then positions the leader or manager for self-analysis.

Confronted with another's point of view, aided by another's perception of him or her, the one who leads or manages supplements his own arsenal of leadership tools. He looks outside himself so that he can more effectively look within himself.

What Do They See When They See You Coming?

What Do They See When They See You Coming? encourages managers to supplement the holster that carries confrontation and correction with a quiver that holds the tools that detect perception. Leadership and management are defined as skills that transcend the temperament and talent of the leader or manager and include awareness of the perception of the one who follows, the one who is being managed, even the one who buys the product or service.

What Do They See When They See You Coming? recognizes that seeking another perception, listening to his or her point of view, mandates awareness of the framework or environment from which another responds. If one seriously seeks the perception of another, one must attempt to understand the breeding grounds of the other's perception. Worded another way, one must ask what it is that influences and determines and forms perception. If perception is a blanket that covers one's thoughts and behavior, then the manager is positioned for a more thorough awareness of perception once he begins to understand the blanket.

Accordingly, *What Do They See When They See You Coming?* will parallel similarities between perception and something that should help the leader or manager understand perception. Therefore, this book is about the blanket that covers one's thoughts and behavior.

Awareness of this blanket is the key that will help you unlock the door that ultimately enables you to understand more thoroughly what they may see when they see you coming, as well as why they may be seeing what they see. Additionally, awareness of this blanket will enable you to consider how you might effectively, with integrity, modify your behavior. The key is the blanket - that which covers the thought and behavior of the one who follows - the employee or the insecure partner.

What Do They See When They See You Coming? seeks to compare this blanket of perception with Thatch. Thatch, that residue of accumulated mown grass, leaves, hay and mulch that blankets the turf and impedes new growth, is compared to the blanket of perception that can equal or even transcend reality. For the purposes of this book, Thatch will equal the blanket of perception that is woven by one's experiences.

The answer to "what they see when they see you coming" will be influenced by their perception, by their Thatch, by their experiences. Throughout the pages of this book, the reader will be encouraged to remember that perception originates not in brick or cedar or wood homes. Perception is not birthed in glass houses. Perception's origin is The Thatch Hut.

If the reader seeks to ask "what they see when they see me coming," the reader must understand that they see from underneath Thatch, they hear from underneath Thatch, they respond from underneath Thatch, they perceive from underneath Thatch!

Specifically, the reader will encounter eight different colors in the kaleidoscope of perception. Worded another way, the reader will explore eight different Thatch-types, eight specific areas in which perception impacts management and leadership.

This book is divided into three sections: The Listening Posts, The Thatch-Types, and The Trail And A Tale.

The book's first section, The Listening Posts, is designed to help you identify the ultimate listening stations. You will be encouraged to remember that your team members reside in and listen from Thatch Huts. They see and perceive you from underneath Thatch.

The second section, The Thatch-Types, certainly the basic nexus of this work, analyzes for the manager eight different types of Thatch. Specifically, this section is structured in such a way as to ask two fundamental questions for each type or subtype: "What does this Thatch-type look like?" "How may I as a manager or leader consider modifying my behavior?"

The third section, The Trail and A Tale, will seek to underscore and elaborate specific steps the manager can take to enable him or her to ask and to respond to our basic question - "What do they see when they see me coming?"

Through every paragraph and page, let us keep our journey's goal in mind. We want to learn to ask and to answer a management question. We are looking for a second opinion - their opinion. We are wanting to factor in their point of view - their perception.

Remember, this is not a textbook. It is certainly not a psychological treatise. In unabashed fashion, this book is presented by a manager for managers. *What Do They See When They See You Coming?* asks a very simple question and seeks to provide possible answers. But again, it is initially an invitation into introspection. It invites the reader to think about what they may be seeing when they see him or her coming.

What Do They See When They See You Coming?

What Do They See When They See You Coming? does not pretend to be a cure-all. It is based to a large degree on hundreds of seminar sessions with corporations and associations.

After having heard numerous stories indicating unintentional excessive confrontation, having heard numerous accounts of avoidance, rejection and downright ignorance of another's perception, I decided it was time to ask the question.

I invite you to do the same.

Part One

The Listening Posts

CHAPTER 1

You Are Not Listening To Me

I t was a cacophony of disharmony. My trauma at the airport had mingled with the frustration of tens of thousands of other passengers.

For me, the difficulty began even before I arrived inside the terminal. As I approached the gate into the parking deck, I noticed several other cars moving toward me - in reverse!

Upon arrival at the gate, I soon observed why so many cars had been backing away from the parking deck's entry. The automatic entry device had malfunctioned. It was impossible to raise the lever that blocked entry.

So, by the hundreds, we backed up this thoroughfare that closely resembled a busy interstate highway. Then we maneuvered our way into the massive, non-decked, general parking area.

Twenty minutes later, I would find an available parking slot. The next thirty minutes would see me and my mammoth suitcase and an extra box of books struggling toward the terminal.

Upon entering the terminal, I hurried to the area that housed the radar detective devices that allowed or denied entry into the concourse transportation system. At this point, I noticed six or eight lines of people. These lines were swelling by the second.

And, that is when I first heard her. She obviously was the general in charge.

Her demeanor lacked any hint of hesitancy or humility. With mechanical precision, she blurted her orders: "Take pen and keys out of both pockets. Place them in the bowl ahead of you."

Most people seemed to be obeying her commands. But then she threw some confusion into the situation: "These lines are for domestic passengers only. If you are flying international, you must move to other lines."

At this point, as the crowd continued to swell, those who were obviously international passengers remained in our line. In frustration, and in a cadence that rivaled a well-functioning machine gun, our general then bellowed, "You are not listening to me. You are not listening to me!"

The amazing, if not somewhat amusing fact, is that most of the international passengers did not speak English and could not understand their general. In frustration, they just continued their forward march.

Now, our general had a response to their subordination. She just spoke louder and repeated her comment more often: "You are not listening to me. You are not listening to me! You are not listening to me!!"

As the confusion and determination of the international passengers increased, so did the volume and intensity of our general's words: "You are not listening to me!!!!"

The truth is, most of the international passengers were listening as well as they could. They just did not speak English. It was our general's perception that they were not listening.

The international passengers saw the general's behavior. They heard her words. They just did not understand the general.

And the general's perception was that they were not listening!

We can hear someone's words and witness their behavior, and they certainly can perceive that we are not listening - even if we are listening.

In our relationships, it is not enough to hear words and observe behavior. It is very important that they perceive that we understand their language. Please remember that their language equals more than their words. It also equals more than their behavior.

It is quite possible that their language significantly includes and indicates their perception. If we are to genuinely understand them, we must seek to comprehend their perception! We must listen for their perception!!

Managers must factor perception into the management equation. Failure to factor their perception into the management equation could create quite a storm!

Brewing A Blizzard!

Georgia has not been the recipient of many blizzards. But, the winter of 1993 seemed to be determined to make up for lost time.

I remember the first day of this experience of biting cold and swirling wind. The reason I remember it so vividly not only relates to the intensity of the storm; I recall the initial onslaught of the blizzard because of something one of our children said, or did not say, on blizzard day number one.

The blizzard was new turf for us all. I had never seen anything like it. What scared me the most was our airwaves were being inundated with warnings. Meteorologists with more than thirty years experience of covering the Atlanta area weather incessantly articulated, "This is the worst ever. Stay inside."

So, when one of our children wanted to slide in the stuff, I immediately and forcefully said, "No!"

When the child increased the intensity of the request, I responded by increasing the force of the denial. All this teenager heard me say was, "No. No to fun!" The teenager felt that I had denied the fun and the teenager did not perceive my caring.

I will never forget what happened. This young teenager started to leave the room in a puff of disappointment and anger, and right before disappearing into the other room, blurted, "Goodbye - goodbye everybody but Dad!"

Dad was bad! Our teenager's perception was that Dad did not care because Dad said no. In reality, Dad was saying "no" because Dad did care. For several hours, the differing perceptions impacted the relationship.

What Do They See When They See You Coming?

Perception can get in the way of communication. Perception is a listening post. It can enhance or destroy communication. Perception can lead to or block relationships. We do not all have the same frame of reference.

Avoidance of this issue is no positive step. To recognize the power of perception – of what they see – even if it is different from reality or from our perception, may help us lead and manage them more effectively.

Remember, even before they began interacting with you, they possess a slant. Their slant, their leaning, will inform their perception. Many a teenager holds to the slant that their parents do not care. They lean toward this line of thinking. This perception of not being cared for can linger forever.

As a leader, how they perceive you is your business. Their frame of reference, their barometer, whether it is a bossy parent, or a callous and excessively confrontational former employer, will inform their inclination toward perception as it relates to you.

It helps if both parties understand the perception of the other. I understood the teenager's perception that I did not care. I did not agree with it, but I understood it. My understanding of that perception enabled me to resist coiling back.

Unfortunately, this is precisely what happens when perception is not factored into the management equation. When I do not ponder what they see, when I refuse to consider their slant, their leaning, their perception, when I obstinately deny their perception, there is a mutual coiling-back. A blizzard is brewing!

The communication lines are downed. Power is cut off. Stagnation replaces communication. Animosity replaces stagnation.

When they feel that you are not listening to them, they may simply perceive that you do not care. The winds of indifference and rejection blow against teammanship and productivity. The team temperature becomes frigid in no time! Failure to listen brews a blizzard!

For the effective manager, the decision to listen mandates attention - not just to what the employee or supervisee says, but attention to why he says it.

This decision to pay listening attention also demands that the manager consider attention in the form of a behavioral response. Behavioral modification by the manager or leader will not always be in order. Sometimes behavioral modification becomes a necessity.

Yes, how they perceive you is your business. And whether or not you choose some sort of behavioral modification is also your business!

What Do They See When They See You Coming?

If you want to prevent a blizzard, or even lessen its intensity, then listen to them. Do not merely listen to their words and their behavior. Hear their perception. Factor in their barometer, their frame of reference.

Listen to their perception. They need your listening. Seek to understand how they feel, even if you do not agree with it. Take a journey in their jogging shoes!

Calming The Storm

The cul-de-sac was my finish line. With ten miles behind me and in me and on me, with ten miles having consumed my whole being and energy, I proudly approached the hill that led to the cul-de-sac. To my thinking, I was, in spite of my exhaustion, attacking that hill with a vigor that I had never before exhibited. I was running amazingly fast - until a four-year-old twerp blurted out from the curb, "Hey mister, how come you are not running very fast?"

My bubble burst - and so did my feet and my legs and the wind beneath my heart!

I did not possess the inclination nor the energy to analyze it then. But later I would ponder that young man's put-down. Quite innocent in nature, his query may have stifled my survival shuffle; but it also ignited my interest in perception.

I found myself wondering about that toddler's frame of reference. I was curious about his barometer. I needed to know with what or with whom he was comparing me.

What he saw when he saw me coming - puffing and panting - was not only influenced by my jogging style and behavior, it was largely determined by his frame of reference.

Ultimately, his comment surfaced from an environment that involved a father - a twenty-eight-year-old whose avocation was participating in and winning marathon races.

The initial reason why my puffing and panting were joined by my pouting was his inquiry about my slow running - when in reality I thought, and still think, I was running rather fast.

The reason I now accept his question more genteelly is that I now understand his barometer, his frame of reference - his muscular, marathon-winning, twenty-eight-year-old speedster of a dad.

His words were humbling, put-downish, and for one of my ilk, accusatory. Initially, I quit running and pouted.

What Do They See When They See You Coming?

But once I listened to his life, once I understood his barometer, his frame of reference, his running with his dad, his perception, then I understood him and his words in a different light. Then, I listened to him. Then, I really listened to him.

Once I factored his perception into my response equation, I understood why he said what he said. Thereafter, what he had said did not have the same impact on me. Once I factored in the power of his perception, I noticed a calming of a storm within me.

"You are not listening to me" may be your invitation to pay more attention, not merely to words and to behavior, but to perception. A positive response to this invitation may assist you in the management and calming of storms.

The persons for whom you seek to provide leadership or management may be crying out for you to listen to them - to listen to their perception.

In order to do this, you must factor in their point of view. To understand their point of view, you must consider their barometer, their frame of reference.

Frames of reference and barometers are listening posts. They are very important listening posts.

Listen, leaders. Listen, managers. How they perceive you is your business!

Perception's Power

You will benefit yourself with awareness of perception's power when you visit perception's breeding place. Perception is birthed at the Thatch point.

The people for whom you seek to provide leadership or management are strongly influenced by this perception factor. How they see you when they see you coming is influenced by this perception factor. How well you will be able to manage or lead them is influenced by this perception factor.

And, this perception factor is controlled by Thatch. Remember, Thatch is perception's breeding place.

An understanding of Thatch will enable you to listen – to really listen – to listen to their perception.

An awareness of Thatch will prevent many a blizzard. Thatch-awareness will calm storms within your team!

CHAPTER 2

The Thatch Hut

We do not reside in brick or stucco or glass houses. We live in Thatch Huts!

My first encounter with Thatch probably occurred forty years ago. As a kindergarten student, I vaguely remember seeing pictures of reed and straw structures that housed people from other lands. This encounter with Thatch was very passive and continues to be a faint reflection for me.

My second encounter with Thatch is current and is experiential in nature. This encounter actually is a battle. I am incessantly waging a war against the accumulated mass of mown grass and matted leaves that constantly carpets and curses my lawn with splotches of brownish gaps.

Just as Thatch stifles and smothers the growth of fescue, so does Thatch impact communication and productivity. The Thatch of this book will not always have a negative impact. But the thrust of this book is that Thatch does impact their perception of you.

Where they have been, the accumulation of their past experiences, the residue of what has happened to them, impacts or informs their perception. And their perception influences what they see when they see you coming!

The past experiences of the ones for whom you seek to provide leadership or management still hang around them and in many cases still dominate them.

It is not the purpose of the manager to eliminate this Thatch. Nor is it necessarily the function of the manager to point out to the employee the employee's Thatch.

The purpose of this book is simply to suggest that managers should be aware that employees live in Thatch Huts.

Each of us breathes from underneath Thatch. The stuff that is our history, the accumulation of our experiences, determines our perception.

Managers, remember that your team members do not merely respond to you on the basis of your words and your behavior. Their response to you is influenced by their Thatch.

What they see when they see you coming is in part determined by their Thatch. They look at you and respond to you from within a Thatch Hut. Their perception, their view, originates within their own Thatch Hut. The residue of their experiences - where they have been - forms a tough Thatch that blankets verbiage and behavior.

Thatch hovers over attitudinal and behavioral responses. Thatch provides a carpet that can enhance or destroy communication and relationships.

To recognize the power of Thatch and perception in communication and in leadership is a powerful first step. The very fact that you have secured this book indicates your seriousness here.

To avoid or to ignore the power of Thatch and perception is to brew a blizzard.

Thatch happens! It happens constantly. The purpose of this book is to remind managers that Thatch happens. Managers, their Thatch does influence what they see when they see you coming.

This author fully understands that one may never completely be able to ascertain what another sees when that other sees one coming. But we can certainly pursue this issue in such a way that our journey will eventually move us closer to at least a better understanding of how others perceive us.

For now, and before we begin to look seriously from a distance, please remember that if you want to know what they see, you have to look out from a Thatch Hut.

Remember, they see you from underneath Thatch. They hear you from underneath Thatch. They respond from underneath Thatch. They perceive you from underneath Thatch. For, after all, they do reside in Thatch Huts.

The perception connection for leaders to ponder is "What do I unnecessarily do that triggers their excessively negative Thatch?"

Past Whiffs

Thirty-one years separated my childhood on Hayes Street from that walk down Prather Bridge Road. Though the roads were within two miles of each other, more than three decades had passed. And I do not believe I had even thought about a persimmon tree during the whole while.

But there it was - not even a stone's throw away from Prather Bridge Road stood a persimmon tree. I must have walked by that tree a thousand times before, but it must have never been bearing fruit before.

But on that day, it was. Persimmons dotted the sidewalk. Some were firm. Some had been squeezed underfoot.

Now, the pressed-down persimmon produces a fragrance like no other. When I smelled "persimmon," I immediately went back thirty-one years.

Though I had not smelled a persimmon for almost a third of a century, the persimmon fragrance was so strong in my catalogue of fragrances that one whiff would be all it would take for me to exclaim, "persimmon!"

You never forget how a persimmon smells. For more than ten years, while we lived on Hayes Street, I was "persimmonized." I would build sand castles, play marbles, search for four-leaf clovers, mow grass, wrestle neighbors, and sleep for 3,650 nights, all within twenty yards of a persimmon tree.

Although I had been separated from that experience by more than three decades, it all came instantly back with one whiff!

What Do They See When They See You Coming?

Their Whiffs Bring Their Stuff Back

Just as my encounter with a persimmon tree on Prather Bridge Road triggered some mixed stuff for me, so do our expressions and our behaviors trigger stuff in others. Their response may be ultimately influenced more by their past whiffs than by the face value of our expressions and our behavior.

It is essential for us to remember that what they see when they see us coming is not only determined by what we express and what we do, but by what their history is. A single persimmon whiff can trigger a whole lot of stuff!

What you express and do is enhanced or distorted by their memory; their whiff with you resurrects past whiffs! In many ways, their past whiffs resemble listening posts!

CHAPTER 3

From A Distance

For several weeks now, our family has been working on a landscaping endeavor in our yard and in the surrounding woods.

One of the teenagers has been most extensively involved; he is quite gifted at structuring borders and clusters. He has developed a particular trait during this series of projects that I trust will benefit him for many experiences to come.

Periodically he stops his work, much of which has taken place at the top of a hill, and walks down the hill. After moving away from the site of labor, he looks up the hill.

What Do They See When They See You Coming?

This perspective of distance has often dictated an enthusiastic "yes - that's it!" On other occasions, his moving away has mandated a change.

Quite often, before he decides to stick with it as it is or opt for a change, he seeks a second opinion.

This book is an invitation to come down from the hill. From a distance, take a gander back up the hill. Examine how things look.

Do you like the way it now is? Do you like what they now see when they see you coming? Do you even know or have a suspicion about what they see?

Should it remain the way it is? Are communication and productivity high on the hill or way down at the bottom? Is your awareness of them and their perception of you as it should be?

Are you confused about which way to go? Have you been asking questions that indicate they are the problem? Would you really like to know how they perceive you? Would you like another opinion about it all? Would you appreciate their point of view?

Then hang with us for about another hour or two. Stay down at the bottom of the hill. Do not hurry back to the top of it all.

From a distance, you can get a better look. And, yes - a second opinion may help.

The Second Opinion

Based on reactions by thousands of seminar participants, it is my suspicion that this introspection from a distance reveals some sort of ambiguity about asking and answering our title question - *What Do They See When They See You Coming?*

Accordingly, our introspection, this inside visit, must mandate an outside visit. Our introspection demands a second opinion - their opinion - what they see!

Here the word "second" should not be interpreted in a way that indicates "second fiddle" or "secondary" or "not as important." The word "second" here simply refers to chronology, to order, to sequential movement.

Normally we first look at things from our perspective and stop there. *What Do They See When They See You Coming?* simply and strongly suggests that we take a second step - a step into their perspective.

It is possible that this step may become so meaningful and beneficial that you eventually will be inclined to consider it a first step into relationships, customer service, parenting, ministry, selling, or leading.

What Do They See When They See You Coming?

If introspection looks within, and if introspection reveals the need to look out, then this second opinion inquiry, this survey into another's perspective, looks out and reveals a possible need for modification of one's own behavior.

To a degree, and only to a degree, their perception, what they see when they see you coming, may enable you to take a first step toward a more effective communication with them.

At this point, it must be understood that the term "communication" is not limited to a meaning that simply indicates an exchange of words. Communication is not bordered by words. Words are not communication's boundaries.

Communication may more closely resemble relationship than it does a mechanical switching of words. Relationship includes attitude, behavior and perception!

It must also be understood that we always have the option to reject the second opinion; but we need to be careful before we do reject it. The whole essence of this book is an encouragement for the reader to seek and respond to the second opinion. But I am well aware that your internal mandate may occasionally indicate a rejection of the second opinion.

For the most part, reception of the second

opinion will at least present you with options you may not have known about before. The second opinion could serve as reassurance. It could lead to realignment. It can be rejected; it can be received!

As you look from a distance into the various Thatch-types, it will be very helpful if you at least consider what surfaces as possible second opinions.

Basically, the eight Thatch-types that will soon surface represent a series of questions. Only you can answer your part of the question. This book gifts you with the perspective of distance and presents you with an opportunity to begin your own contemplation.

The eight colors in the kaleidoscope of perception that follow, the eight Thatch-types, represent the issues that have most often surfaced in our sessions with corporations and associations. Please be very sure to understand that there is out there within the large workforce of our nation the perception that some managers do not even bother to ask, much less answer, our title question. There is out there in the workplace the perception that, in some cases, workers are little more than tools to be manipulated; rarely are some of them considered as persons to be understood.

I must state that though this perception is out there, it is not the only perception out there. Thousands of managers and leaders do legitimately value and encourage their employees. It is my pleasure to work with many of them.

Many managers labor to ascertain the perception of supervisees. The number of managers who legitimately care is legion!

But still there is an opportunity for improvement. From a distance, aided by their possible second opinion, let us see if we can address this opportunity.

We have just examined the key listening posts of frame of reference and barometer. There are certainly other key listening posts ranging from serious eye contact focused in on another's transparency, to questions intended to verify reception of the message between source and receiver. But for our purposes, listening posts, and for that matter look-out towers, have much to do with barometers, or measuring sticks, or frames of reference - Thatch.

Soon we will examine these Thatch-types - the kaleidoscope of the eight colors of perception. Before we delve further into these Thatch-types, it will be helpful to seek to understand how we will be looking at Thatch, what we will be looking for, and why we should ponder our response.

To help us, we will need a special listening tool!

CHAPTER 4

The Thatch Scope

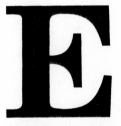arlier this week, I planned to ask one of the children a particular question. I had hoped and even assumed that the answer might provide me with a helpful way to introduce this very chapter. So, when I picked him up at the bus stop, I immediately popped the question, "What do you call the thing that helps soldiers see at night?" I also mentioned that the answer might help me write a part of this book.

He suggested that the device might be called some sort of infrared-assisted nightscope. But he did not drop the issue at that point.

Now, you must understand that this young

man's entrepreneurial spirit is quite intense. On several occasions, I have given him pocket change to affirm and reward his innovations and contributions.

Not only did I notice his excitement that I would ask him a question that might give him an opportunity to help with the book, I immediately detected a mental churning that indicated he was already pondering the possibility of additional pocket change.

"I can go to the library tomorrow and look up the exact name," he suggested.

"That will be fine. Let me know how long it takes," I responded.

Well, it took a long time, a very long time!

I am grateful that his mother went with him, otherwise he might have stayed much longer. But, eight books later, encouraged by his mother, he was ready to leave. I imagine the two librarians who had assisted him were also ready for him to leave. I further imagine that even the periodical computer breathed a sigh of relief when he departed. He and his mother examined the eight books, and prodded by her encouragement, he checked out just four books.

I was surprised, if not amazed, that several books contained material that related to this particular perception-of-night tool. As I now understand it, this genre of devices aimed at enhancing vision at night includes night-vision goggles.

For the purposes of this book, our Thatch scope, our Thatch goggles, look beyond the nebulous and ambiguous night of perception and provide at least some parcel of clearer vision.

When we improve our Thatch vision, we come closer to an understanding of the power of perception over reality. When we are able to see and ponder and consider their Thatch, we are better able to focus in on what they see when they see us coming.

Our Thatch scope enables us to detect eight different colors in the kaleidoscope of perception. Our Thatch scope or Thatch goggles will in reality include a listening tool as well as a Thatch-view finder.

Our scope for Thatch, designed to help us see and hear how they may be influenced in their perception, positions us for investigation into what they see when they see us coming.

If you thoroughly understand that how they perceive you is your business, then you will eventually appreciate the Thatch scope that will help you ponder the blanket of their experiences, the accumulation of the mown grass of their lives - their perception. You can call it a Thatch scope or you can call it Thatch goggles. Either way, it will help you ask and seek to answer two specific questions about the Thatch-type of perception.

It will be helpful if we understand the structure of questions used in scoping each of the Thatch-types!

The Structure

In reference to each Thatch-type or subtype, we will ask and seek to answer two questions: What does this Thatch-type look like? How might I consider modifying my behavior in response to it?

Remember the issue is our title - *What Do They See When They See You Coming?* For our purpose, Thatch is the thread that holds together the perception connection.

It will be helpful for us to analyze the two questions that will enable us to clarify and respond to this thread!

The First Leg – What?

What does it look like?

Basically this question should lead to other questions that describe what they may be seeing when this particular Thatch-type is triggered: What am I doing that might be triggering this Thatch-type? If they are perceiving me in a certain way in relationship to this issue, what do they think they are seeing? If my behavior unnecessarily disturbs them and triggers a negative Thatch response, precisely what does my behavior look like? How is it manifest? How does this Thatch-type filter and flavor people's responses and perceptions?

The Second Leg – How?

How can I respond?

How might I consider modifying my behavior so that what they see will more closely resemble what I really prefer them to see? How can I consider modifying my behavior in such a way that I, on the one hand, will remain faithful to my own internal mandates but, on the other hand, be considerate of and responsive to their perception? What can I do in precise fashion that will enable me to respond effectively to their point of view, to their perception? What procedures can I practice that will enable me routinely to consider, to factor in, and to respond effectively to their perception?

Remember, if you ask the right questions, you might receive the appropriate answers. The questions are merely important first steps. Fail to ask the questions, the answers never come!

The First Step

Ask most people what they remember about The Ed Sullivan Show and they will probably recall Elvis' eventual appearance, the Beatles, or Mr. Sullivan's diminutive neck.

My strongest recollection of Mr. Sullivan's show travels back to a Sunday night. The event took place more than thirty years ago.

Sophie Tucker was Mr. Sullivan's guest. All I remember about her appearance was something she sang about taking a first step and then going all the way. But for some reason, that has remained indelibly printed into the rolodex of my mind.

The first steps are the crucial ones!

Almost three years from the day this very chapter is being written, the 1996 Olympics are to arrive in Atlanta. Before Atlanta was announced to the world as "Host City," Atlanta had to take first steps.

Before Henry Aaron hit his record-breaking seven hundred and fifteenth homerun, he had to take a first step, hit his first homerun.

The Power Of Perception Over Reality

Just last week, our family visited Key West, Florida. The nucleus of this trip would be two fishing excursions into the sea. One day would yield two sailfish. Both were safely released back into their mother ocean. A second day would produce a catch of snapper and grouper.

That second day began with another sort of catch. The first hour on the boat saw us catching us our bait - much smaller fish. Our first step, before we caught the big ones, was to catch the little ones.

Before you really make the big perception connection, you must first seek to answer two little questions: What does this Thatch-type look like? How can I respond?

Asked time and again, the small questions - the what and the how - become the first step toward making the perception connection.

These questions become the first step toward an understanding of the power of perception over reality. Each Thatch-type, and in most cases each subtype, will be assigned a reminder formula and a perception connection question that will help you remember and utilize specific points in relationship to the particular perception connection.

Always remember that an understanding of the Thatch-type will enable you to more closely ask

What Do They See When They See You Coming?

and answer our basic title question - *What Do They See When They See You Coming?*

    With Thatch scope in mind, let us now pursue our eight Thatch-types of perception.

Part Two

The Thatch-Types

CHAPTER 5

Personality

The Pain

That door drives me crazy! Positioned on the side of the mall entrance, this door leads to one of our town's largest department stores. For decades, it has clearly been marked "pull." And for forty years, I have been trying to push it open. It should have been a "push" door.

When a push door is labeled "pull," it leads to pain for the ones seeking to enter through it. Tension develops when push meets pull.

Without delving into the complex nature of a plethora of personality profiles, one can simply state that the differences among us can sometimes be equaled with the disparity between a push and a pull.

What Do They See When They See You Coming?

For our purposes, if you are a pull door, please think of the push doors in your organization. Worded another way, please ponder those personalities among you that vastly differ from your own personality.

When there is interaction between you as a pull door and them as a push door, it is possible that they sense tension. More importantly, it is even possible that they perceive you as one who relishes in creating and participating in this tension.

The question I lift up for consideration here is a simple one - Do they, your team members, particularly ones with personality styles opposite from yours, perceive you as one who thrives on confrontation? You can also ask this question about those with whom you share similar personality styles.

The reminder formula here is: A push plus a pull can equal a pain. The perception connection question here is: Do they perceive you as thriving on confrontation?

What Does Thriving On Confrontation Look Like?

It looks like a bully!

I had to look "bully" up in a dictionary to be sure I was spelling it correctly. I did not find it necessary to look up "bully" in order to understand the meaning of the word.

Skinny toddlers and teenagers know painfully well the meaning of the word "bully." Those chosen last to play neighborhood football, those denied the blessing of bulging biceps and gifted coordination, know full well the meaning of "bully."

A bully is not merely one who confronts others into a verbal or physical fight. The bully is the one who appears to thrive on the fight.

Thriving on confrontation looks very much like a bully enjoying demeaning or actually hurting another. And thriving on confrontation looks its best, or its worst, when crowds are present. Crowds seem to elicit the anger and the adrenaline and the performance of the bully.

I cannot recall a time when I was bullied by another without a crowd being present. Crowds draw forth the bully's worst venom.

Thriving on confrontation looks like showcasing, attention getting, bullying! Thriving on confrontation looks like anger that is sabotaged or redirected. Worded another way, thriving on confrontation looks like diversion - I cannot get what I want or need this way, so I will try it this way. Thriving on confrontation gives the impression that the entire process is actually being enjoyed by the bully.

As far as management teams and their staffs are concerned, thriving on confrontation has several faces. Over the past decade, I have worked with hundreds, if not thousands, of management teams. I have observed thriving on confrontation to take on looks that range from physical fights to verbal jostling. I have noticed thriving on confrontation to take on appearances that range from pouting on public pity pots to the issuance of internal memos loaded with nasty innuendos.

Thriving on confrontation can look like a fight or a fuss; it can resemble an incessant and open pouting or a more clandestine, yet subtlety obvious, stabbing behind the back.

If someone perceives you as thriving on confrontation, they may perceive that you seem to enjoy bullying them in what they consider to be their own backyard. Thriving on confrontation can look like an excessive and unnecessary request to do it again and again, even when the first result was much more than adequate. Thriving on confrontation can equally resemble an unreasonable request to finish a task within an utterly impossible timeframe.

Just last week, I was speaking for a risk management society. I was in a rush to catch a plane when two young ladies indicated a need to share with me the difficulty of their tasks.

I particularly remember one of the ladies relating that whenever she indicated that the timeframe for an accomplishment of a task assigned to her was unusually short and difficult, her supervisor would simply take issue with her time management skills.

Granted, a supervisee can reveal a thriving on confrontation by poorly managing time. But certainly the supervisor can also exhibit thriving on confrontation by demanding the accomplishment of a task within an unreasonable framework of time and then accusing the subordinate of ineffective time management if it is not all consummate by the deadline.

Thriving on confrontation manifests itself in the gifted student who refuses to study at all, hand in assignments, show up for class. Thriving on confrontation manifests itself in a teenager who uses foul language precisely because his parents find such language distasteful. Thriving on confrontation manifests itself in the worker who fuels rumor mills in an effort to frustrate a supervisor. It shows up as arrogance in some, as anger in others. It resembles controversy and pettiness. It can actually lead to emotional and physical harm. Thriving on confrontation can equal an incessant invitation for attention.

It must be clearly stated that thriving on confrontation is a learned skill or curse. Many thrive on confrontation because they have learned how to do it so well. And, they have been well rewarded for doing it well.

If this thriving can be learned, then it can be modified. It can be rewarded; we can attempt to reject it.

Unfortunately, many people have experienced so much Thatch related to thriving on confrontation that they have difficulty rejecting it when we serve it to them again. Many thrive on confrontation because it is something they learned to do in the Thatch, and their Thatch still has power over them. Others will quickly perceive another as thriving against them because the past whiffs of their Thatch involved others who thrived in confrontation toward them.

Thriving on confrontation happens because it has been compensated. It got for us what we wanted.

As a manager, I must understand that they thrive on confrontation sometimes, and sometimes so do I. It is particularly important that I understand that my thriving on confrontation brings back to them negative past whiffs out from their Thatch Huts, out from their experiences. When I do something that they perceive as thriving on confrontation, I have pulled a switch that may have as its origin something that occurred decades ago - in their history!

If it is possible that when they see you coming, they see one who thrives on confrontation, then you may want to ponder behavioral modification.

How Does One Who Thrives On Confrontation Modify?

Granted, modification may not be necessary at all here. But the whole purpose of this book is to invite introspection. If modification is mandated in your circumstances, if you would like to consider modification of excessively confrontational behavior, then you may want to ponder the following three behavioral modifications:

1. Listen more and talk less.
2. Praise more and condemn less.
3. Bless yourself more and curse yourself less.

Listen More And Talk Less

Listening tends to lead toward an environment that is less confrontational in nature. Excessive talk can be both selfish and obnoxiously aggravating.

Please remember that in one way or another we are all insecure. Many times, our exceptionally insecure team members may perceive our excessive talking as an incessant counter to their need and right to express themselves. The more we talk, and the less we listen, the more confrontational we are perceived to be. The sheer volume of our words is perceived as possible confrontation. Each additional word out of our mouths can become an additional bullet out of the arsenal of confrontation.

Please understand that it may not be only the bitter and accusatory nature of our words that is confrontational. The sheer volume of the number of words, the quantity of our words, may be perceived as confrontational - a denial of their right to express themselves.

Leading has to do with their point of view. Though their point of view is certainly not the only point of view, nor the ultimate point of view, it is a point of view you may want to consider. How can you consider it if you do not hear it? Listen!

It is my experience that customers do not so much rebel against mistakes as they retaliate against a nonchalant and nonresponsive attitude about the mistake by the salesperson or by the customer service agent. Similarly, your employee or supervisee may not so much rebel at the fact that you do not ultimately pursue what their point of view indicates, as they will retaliate against your nonchalant and nonresponsive attitude about their point of view. It may not be the fact that you did not follow their point of view that drives them crazy. What may bother them the most, what they may perceive as utterly confrontational, may be the fact that you did not even indicate a willingness to listen to their point of view. Talk less. Listen more.

Listen; do not patronize. Do not merely pretend to pay attention to the motions of listening. Pay attention to the one talking.

Remember, we are transparent. And superficial listening may deny the insecure partner's point of view more than not listening at all. Superficial listening is very destructive. Superficial listening may indicate a hidden agenda that closes doors between parties rather than opening the door toward communication.

Talk less. Genuinely listen more. Appropriate behavioral modification may include attentive listening.

Praise More, Condemn Less

This theme will surface repeatedly throughout this book. What they may see when they see you coming may be someone very gifted at catching them doing wrong! What they may see when they see you coming may be someone who appears inept at catching them doing right!

If they perceive the instances in which you confront to far outweigh the circumstances in which you praise them, they may perceive you as confrontational. Worded another way, if the frequency and intensity of your corrective statements is more than the frequency and intensity of your affirmations, they may perceive you as confrontational. If they perceive you as always trying to catch them doing wrong, and rarely trying to catch them doing right, they may perceive you as confrontational.

"He is always on my case" may be her way of saying, "He seems to thrive on confrontation!"

"I never seem to be able to please him" may be his way of articulating the confrontational behavior of a supervisor. The supervisor appears to thrive on his own displeasure.

"More is never enough" may be someone else's way of saying, "No matter what I do, no matter how much I do, he always finds fault, something wrong, something missing. There seems always to be something for him to confront. It is almost as if he enjoys doing it!"

Throwing some genuine affirmations into the mix may be appropriate behavioral modification at this point.

Log It

It may be very helpful for you to log your confrontation-praise ratio. This has proven to be exceptionally enlightening to many of our managers.

Of course, it is highly important that you always remember never to assume that they know that you feel appreciation or praise toward them. Unfortunately, most of us confront weaknesses much more than we affirm strengths - even if we have feelings about both. Remember here you are not logging the number of times you feel confrontational, as opposed to the number of times you feel appreciative. You are logging the ratio between the times you behave out your confrontation in relationship to the times you behave out your praise.

Measure It

Not only should you analyze the mix of confrontations to affirmations, you should seek to measure for yourself the intensity and specificity of your confrontations in relationship to the intensity and specificity of your affirmations.

Unfortunately, most of us bless our confrontational or corrective statements with a particular vigor. We curse our statements of affirmation with a bland stoicism.

If their Thatch includes a past whiff of someone who never praised them, they may be inclined to pick up on any tendency you have to confront with frequency and intensity. They will also be able to detect easily the rarity and indifference of your affirmations.

Possible behavioral modification may include an examination of your confrontational-affirmational ratio. It will help if you learn to log and measure it!

Bless Yourself More, Curse Yourself Less

Remember that the umbrella for this Thatch-type is the personality. There is not a suggestion here that we change our personalities. Again, one must bear in mind throughout the reading of this book that these pages are only suggestions. This book is written by a manager for managers. Its purpose is to ask questions and to encourage managers to think. But the ultimate suggestion here is not personality change. However, the reader is encouraged to ponder possible behavioral modification.

If what they see when they see you coming is one who talks more than he listens, one who confronts more than he praises, then you may want to ponder why you exhibit behavior that is so self-centered and confrontational.

One answer you may want to think about is possibly related to the way you treat yourself!

Speaking as a business manager, and as one who has worked in seminars with thousands of other managers, let me suggest that it is often my observation that we are confrontational toward others because we are so excessively confrontational with ourselves. We supply ourselves with a constant menu of confrontation. The confrontational level of our blood exceeds normal and borderline levels and becomes a risk in that it reaches the point where it is likely to surface from within and exit without - toward others.

What Do They See When They See You Coming?

If my nutrition is confrontation toward myself, then my behavior is likely to be confrontational. If my frame of reference is self-confrontation, if I habitually confront myself, I am likely to, out of habit, confront others.

It is not as if there is a limit to the confrontation arsenal. Do not argue that you can spend all of your confrontational dollars on yourself and not have any left to spend on others.

To the contrary, confrontation is highly reproductive and expansive in nature. The supply does not diminish with use, it magnifies with use. If my diet is confrontation, confrontation is routinely consumed and digested. The confrontation that I plug into myself will become a contagion that is eventually spread out toward others. It is as if I become what I eat. If I digest enough confrontation toward myself, I will become confrontational toward others.

If I am so harsh and confrontational toward myself that I become infected with confrontation, I become highly contagious and vent my own confrontation toward others.

The Antidote

The behavioral modification that must be contemplated here is some sort of counteraction, a degree of response to the problem, that is curative, or at least helpful in nature - an antidote.

An antidote presented for your consideration is a healthy dose of self-appreciation. Is that not at least worth a try?

If you have stuck with this exceedingly long chapter, if you are still embarking through these rather heavy pages, then you may be seriously considering the possibility that what they see when they see you coming may indeed be confrontational in nature. Granted, what they see will have a great deal to do with their focus, their Thatch, where-they-have-been, their past whiffs. But what they see may also be directly related to your confrontational behavior.

If you think that they may be right when they think you thrive on confrontation, is it not worth considering thriving on something else?

Focus on your strengths more, and focus on your weaknesses less. You may find your outward focus toward others taking an about face. You may find yourself focusing on their strengths more and their weaknesses less.

Concentrate on listening to your deep inner voice more; you may become inclined to listen more effectively to them.

Quietly and sincerely praise yourself more, program praise within and praise may eventually burst out toward them. If inner harshness breeds outer harshness, then inner softness may breed outer softness. Acceptance of yourself may be the antidote that corrects excessive confrontation and leads toward a more genuine acceptance of others.

Constantly battle within and you will find yourself eventually and constantly battling without - toward them. Praise yourself more often, curse yourself less often, and you will find that the same sort of praise may start being exhibited toward them.

If excessive confrontation is the disease, a dose of self-acceptance may be a first-step antidote toward a reversal of a thriving on confrontation.

The Reality

If the first subtype underneath the personality Thatch-type relates to thriving on confrontation, the second subtype relates to the denial of one's uniqueness.

The reminder formula here is: A team minus a mold equals a reality. The perception connection question is: Do they perceive you as denying their uniqueness?

Though far fewer pages will be given to this subtype than were given to its brother-type, thriving on confrontation, this issue does merit attention.

What we quite often see in our management seminars and conferences is a quiet rebellion against superiors who deny the uniqueness of middle managers!

Recognizing that teams ultimately equal unity in diversity rather than an exclusive and self-debasing mold, these middle managers seem to be expressing their right to a degree of individuality.

The Cloning Rebellion

Earlier in this book, I referred to a family fishing trip deep into Florida. You may recall that within a period of an hour, we caught two sailfish. As I understand it, there is now some foundation that is encouraging the safe release of these beautiful, proud, and exceptionally independent fish. Our captain supported this effort. Accordingly, and with little reservation, we agreed to release our sailfish.

As the first fish was being reeled in, and considerably prior to release-time, the mate asked me if I would be interested in having a picture taken of the fish so that an exact replica could be made and shipped back to Georgia for exhibition on a prominent wall.

I was totally caught off guard by his suggestion and responded that I did not think that would be necessary. I must also admit that later, when the second sailfish was caught, I was very glad I had not agreed to have a replica made of the first fish. What I had done for one teenager, I would certainly have had to do for the second.

But there certainly was a rebellion within me toward the replica. The rebellion was not merely financial in nature. It was a rebellion that indicated a quest for authenticity, for proud individuality.

If there was going to be a fish on the wall, and I must admit there was not a big desire for such a thing, then it certainly should have been the real one. The replica would certainly not have sufficiently reproduced the event. The duplicate would have been a dud.

In similar fashion, middle managers rebel within against the move to make them simply a replica of the real thing - the boss!

Duplicates Become Duds

It is my experience that duplicates, or replicates, delete authenticity. Authenticity cannot be cloned. Uniqueness cannot be duplicated. Duplicates do become duds.

What Does The Denial Of Uniqueness Look Like?

It looks like a duplicate. It looks like a dud. It looks like a replica. It looks like something less than real, less than authentic; it looks like cloning.

And it is not always smart! I do not do my best as I duplicate you. I do not perform most effectively when I am a replica of you.

Oh certainly, there is a fabric, a theme, a constancy to a team - and there should be!

But this theme, this focus, does not mandate denial of one's uniqueness!

To the contrary, I can most effectively carry your mast when I am myself. If you want me to thrust out on your behalf, allow me some latitude for flipping and flopping in my best style. Denial of my uniqueness looks like your demanding that I swish and swash just as you want everyone else to swish and swash.

Surely, you as employer have the right to create structure and focuses. But if you want her to help you most effectively, you do not want her to see you as one who merely demands duplicates, reaches for replicas or chooses clones!

Remember, for your company, duplicates ultimately become duds. If a dud is a shell that will not explode, a cloned employee is one who will not ultimately do his or her best.

How Does One Modify Uniqueness Denial?

If your people consider you as one who denies their uniqueness, and if you think there may be some merit in their thinking, then you may want to consider some or all of the following behavioral modification steps:

1. Match needs to skills.
2. Re-evaluate needs-skill mix.
3. Encourage uniqueness.
4. Exhibit uniqueness.

Match Needs To Skills

If one could measure the intensity of head-nodding in my seminars, it would reach maximum level at this point. Perhaps I should make clear here that head-nodding equals not a dozing off but an energetic agreement. What I say is simple, "It is an issue of preventative medicine. We would have fewer problems if we initially matched our needs with their skills." The enthusiastic agreement on the part of the audience is intense and complex.

One head-nodder agrees because he hired a person as a customer service representative before he recognized that that person detested dealing with conflict. Another agrees because she hired a person as a trainer before discerning that the person literally could not speak in public. A third agrees with my statement because he personally has been cast into a mold that requires less of him than he wants to give.

If you want to deal with their perception that you deny their uniqueness, then seek to prevent other similar problems before they occur. Seek to match the needs, tasks or requirements of a job with the interest, talents or capabilities of the employee.

There is a plethora of personality profile tools that will help you here. A simple interview aimed at securing an inventory of the skills and interests of a particular prospective employee will also help you.

If their past whiffs, their Thatch, reveal a predisposition against cloning, watch out. Be sure to match your needs with their skills.

Re-evaluate Needs-Skills Match

Sometimes we are wrong. Sometimes the match was not appropriate. Realignment may be in order.

You do not change tires everytime your car needs realignment. You realign so you will not have to change tires.

If your people possibly perceive you as denying their uniqueness, do not automatically change people. Realign!

If the first match was inappropriate, seek to do better. Suggest realignment.

There Is A Side Benefit

As this particular section is being written, I am thinking of one of my clients - one of the country's largest utility companies. They are constantly re-aligning their people - matching again and again changing needs with developing skills.

The end result of this realignment is that they are building for the team diverse, multi-experienced, multi-skilled, middle managers capable of becoming upper managers.

Realignment not only builds a better match. Realignment builds leaders exposed to various levels of operation. All the while this re-evaluation, this realignment, seeks to quench the thirst for authenticity. This realignment seeks to fuel the quest for pursuing and exhibiting one's uniqueness.

Encourage Uniqueness

Behavioral modification at this point does not simply equal acceptance of uniqueness. It transcends passive acceptance and approaches active encouragement. Behavioral modification is not only reactive in that it moves from cloning to accepting. It is deliberately innovative in that it moves from accepting to encouraging uniqueness.

Managers, please remember that you encourage the uniqueness of another personality when you allow for that uniqueness, acknowledge that uniqueness, affirm that uniqueness and reward that uniqueness.

The Breakdown Of
Uniqueness-Encouragement

Allow

Create an environment where uniqueness is allowed. It is to become clear to all team participants that uniqueness is accepted.

Your team members are informed that it is appropriate to bring their unique skills to the task.

Acknowledge

They are encouraged by the very fact that you notice. They are discouraged by the very fact that you fail to notice.

Let them become aware that you have observed their "specialness."

Affirm

You move beyond allowance and acknowledgment toward affirmation. Affirmation equals both verbal support and other expressions of encouragement. Affirmation equals a smile, a note, your time.

Reward

Selectively administered, and as a natural extension of allowance, acknowledgment and affirmation, rewarding uniqueness validates the seriousness of your encouragement. The reward does not have to be complex.

Last month, I spoke for one of the state's largest school systems. I normally speak for a particular school system's teachers or honor graduates. On this occasion, and for the first time ever, I spoke for the annual appreciation banquet for this system's bus drivers.

All the reward the drivers received was a sheet of paper, some barbecue blessed with a special sauce, and me. It did not take much to bring them out in tremendous numbers.

But one by one, they were encouraged for their uniqueness and the special way they greeted and safely transported and dismissed precious young ones.

Exhibit Uniqueness

If you are going to elicit their uniqueness, then you will want to exhibit your own uniqueness. If your team ultimately reaches its goal only when one by one your team members exhibit uniqueness, then your team members will be encouraged to exhibit that uniqueness when they observe your example.

Behavioral modification here is the exhibition of uniqueness that does not deny another's, it enhances another's uniqueness. It is as if you begin to say, "I invite you to be unique. It is appropriate to be unique. Even I choose to be unique."

Exhibit your own uniqueness more, and you will be noticing fewer efforts to clone, fewer attempts to produce replicas and duplicates, and more inclinations to breed uniqueness.

Exhibit your own uniqueness, and you will be better positioned to match their unique skills to your needs. Exhibit your own uniqueness, and you will be better positioned to allow, acknowledge, affirm and reward their uniqueness. Excessively hold your own uniqueness in, it will ooze out in such a camouflaged way that it may actually resemble the denial of another's uniqueness.

Let it out! Let your uniqueness out; you will resemble a proud, authentic sailfish, eliciting the unique flipping and flopping of other proud and authentic sailfish.

Exhibit your uniqueness, and when they see you coming they may see you, not as one who demands the denial of their uniqueness, but as one who is free to allow others their right to be unique.

When the exhibition of your uniqueness elicits their uniqueness, there is a mutually beneficial relationship for you and your team.

The Nexus

As I close this chapter, let me encourage you to feel comfortable to visit it, this very chapter, again and again. It is by far, and by intention, the longest chapter of the book. By book's end, you may perceive it to be one of the ultimate Thatch-types for your consideration.

Viewing out of the Thatch Hut that is their personality, they may be inclined to perceive you as thriving on confrontation and denying their uniqueness. To ask what they see when they see you coming at these spots, the very spots of thriving on confrontation and denying uniqueness, may literally position you for a more thorough understanding of the whole of this book.

CHAPTER 6

Persistence

The Double-Fault

Miss two serves in a row and the tennis world will say you have "double-faulted." Fail to understand the power of persistence as it emanates out of the Thatch Hut and you will double-fault.

The reminder formula for this subtype relating to persistence is: serves minus follow-throughs equal double-faults. The perception connection question is: Do they perceive you as flippant?

Unfortunately, many managers issue directives that include the promissory note of action or reaction on their part. They serve out promises and fail to follow through. The result is a double-fault of perceived incompetency and flippancy. They issue mixed signals. There is conflict or tension between what they indicate on the one hand and what they actually do on the other hand.

Stop And Go At The Same Time

Just last week, we were checking out a location for an upcoming seminar. Approximately two miles from the seminar site, there was a road repair crew servicing the road. Traffic was being intermittently halted.

The flow of traffic was being controlled by an elderly gentleman. He was assisted by a sign that he held. On one side of the sign was the word "stop." The other side indicated "slow." His purpose was to hold the sign toward the traffic in such a way that the traffic knew whether to "stop" or go in response to "slow."

At the particular moment in question, our car was the only vehicle on our side of the road. The gentleman incessantly held "stop" in front of me. After several moments, he indicated with his free hand that I should start moving. But he did not change his sign. With one hand, he was positioning a "stop" sign directly toward me. With the other hand, he was motioning for me to move forward, to go.

I looked toward him and his mixed signals. I looked at my wife and her understanding smile. I looked all around to see what might really be the safe thing to do. Finally, we moved in response to his waving hand, ignoring his "stop" sign.

The gentleman was serving a "stop" sign. He was following through with a hand motion that invited movement!

What Does Flippancy Look Like?

As I understand it, flippancy indicates a behavior that is shallow and pert. Behavior that is flippant is trifling. It indicates a lack of seriousness, a frivolousness, because it is inconsistent.

Flippant behavior indicates a jerky, "flip-floppish" sort of relationship between attitude and behavior, between verbiage and action.

Because there is inconsistency between our signals, shallowness or even incompetency may be perceived. This lack of seriousness, this apparent indication of insignificance, actually becomes significantly serious!

Do you hold up, in a plethora of ways, one sort of sign for your people? Do your hand and body and heart motions indicate a movement that is counter to the "sign" you give? Is it possible that your mixed signals, the mixture that can indicate a lack of seriousness or a degree of insignificance, may be perceived by them as a lack of interest on your part?

How Does One Modify Perceived Flippant Behavior?

If some of this rings true for you, there are three behavioral modification steps that you may want to ponder:

1. Acknowledge your transparency.
2. Consider their transparency.
3. Verify the integrity of the message.

Acknowledge Your Transparency

If you want them to see that you are firm and persevering in the directions and statements that you serve out toward them, then you must understand afresh that you speak with "forked tongue" if your actions do not validate your words.

Due to your transparency, they can see into you, beyond your words, in such a way that they can detect whether you mean what you say, whether you follow through.

If you desire an enduring and positive relationship between your words and your actions, acknowledge the fact that your team members not only hear your words, they observe the "proof in the pudding" - your behavior.

Worded another way, they can see right through your words - to your behavior - to your follow-through. Acknowledge your transparency!

Acknowledge Their Transparency

And you can, to a degree, see through their words. Their transparency, their behavior, can indicate whether or not they perceive you as flippant.

Their frustration with your inconsistency can be manifest by their own inconsistency. If your flippancy indicates that you take something in less than a serious fashion, they may mirror your lack of seriousness and attach the label of "insignificant" to a project.

When I go on site to speak for a corporation, I can immediately detect whether or not there is a serious inconsistency, an absence of the "follow-through" within management, by what I observe within the team.

If you think you may have a persistence perception problem, look outward - look toward them.

Their personhood, their performance, may be mirroring your flippancy.

What you see when you look outward may indicate what they see when they look outward - toward you. This marriage of the outward glances may mandate that you look within for inconsistency.

Are they mirroring your flippancy? You can tell. You can acknowledge their transparency. The way they behave may be telling you something about yourself. The way they behave may be indicating what they see when they see you coming!

Verify The Integrity

If the Thatch of their past whiffs indicates an allergic reaction against flippancy, you can seriously seek to verify the integrity of your message.

If integrity is some degree of a consistent correspondence within and out from oneself, you can verify the constancy between your orders, your statements, your memos and your behavior. There are several ways to achieve this constancy.

Ask For An Answer

The first method of course is to ask for an answer. There are many managers who have found this method exceptionally helpful. Granted, it is a daring move and the respondees may be very guarded in their answer statements.

But, if you sincerely want to learn whether or not they perceive an inconsistency between your serves and your follow-throughs, ask them. If you are concerned about a guarded or weighted response from subordinates, send out open-ended questionnaires that demand no signature. Or ask superiors or persons on the periphery to share their opinion about any possible inconsistency within you. Some may just share some very helpful data at this point.

Observe Them

A second step that could provide some verification of the degree of integrity between your serves and your follow-throughs may be a thorough reading of your team members.

Remember, quite often their persistency factor, their integrity between thought expression and behavioral extension, mirrors your own persistency factor.

Assure Authenticity

A third procedure that could insure some verification between thought and action, between serves and follow-throughs, is authenticity assurance.

A program designed toward authentic correspondence in relationships between procedures and actions, promises and follow-throughs, indications and substantiations, will benefit you.

Simply worded, you organize a system, an authenticity assurance program, that would be as fundamental as a log or as complex as a computer-assisted tracking advice that enables you to monitor and correct inconsistencies between serves and follow-throughs.

It is my experience that simply creating some follow-through monitoring device, however simple or complex, indicates awareness of a red flag of perceived flippancy. After awareness is achieved, much of the rest of this will take care of itself as long as you seek to establish some sort of program that will provide you with an opportunity to monitor the progress of your responses.

The Broken Spirit

The enigma of the broken spirit is often best defined and explained by the accumulation of hurtful experiences. When superiors or cohorts constantly revisit our mistakes and shortcomings, we become frazzled and worn down. It is as if time enhances rather than diminishes the focus of their memory.

We do something wrong or ineffectively and they seem to remember it extremely well. They persistently remember!

We do something well and they seem to forget quickly. They persistently forget!

The reminder formula here is: Beaten dead horses equal broken spirits. The perception connection question is: Do they perceive you as remembering too well and too long?

What Does Remembering Too Well Look Like?

I helped pay my way through college by working as a disc jockey at a radio station in Macon, Georgia. One advantage of this job was the fact that it allowed for study during the air shift, if one was assigned the late night or extremely early morning shift.

What Do They See When They See You Coming?

During these shifts, the number of listeners was lower; the commercial level was almost nonexistent; the boss was asleep; and you could segue records!

You could simply select an album, preferably a multi-artist disk, and let it roll. And, you could study!

Late one night, I had placed on turntable number one an exceptionally long album, but it seemed to be running longer than normal. I did not bother to check it and continued pursuing the disparity between macro and micro economics - until the phone rang.

The boss was as hot as Bibb County's one hundred plus degree weather. "The doggone needle is stuck, you dummy! Do something," he exclaimed as he hung up the phone.

Well, I did something. I adjusted the needle and eventually changed albums. I quit studying, and I learned a significant lesson in broadcasting. I must have interjected twenty-five weather forecasts, fifteen time checks and numerous artist-fact bits over the next two hours.

Remembering too well looks like "the doggone needle getting stuck" on mistakes, stuck on shortcomings, stuck on remembering errors too well and too long. The same confrontational innuendos and phrases are incessantly repeated.

Just as the radio station owner became hot, so do our team members become heated in frustration when we incessantly beat dead horses. Dead horses equal issues they thought, obviously in error, had already been addressed and forgotten. It is music, often painful in nature, that has already been played once and is now unmercifully being beaten into their ears and heads and spirits.

Rub their mistakes into their faces long enough, and you will soon observe that they possess broken spirits. A broken spirit can resemble apathy or rebellion. It can impact your team members physically and emotionally.

Beating dead horses bursts bubbles, produces pessimism and squelches spontaneity!

When the needle gets stuck on a dead horse, you need to do something!

How Do You Modify When You Remember Mistakes Too Well?

If you are occasionally the on-duty announcer or supervisor who allows the needle to become persistently stuck on a dead horse, an issue that had already been resolved, already been played once, there are two behavioral modification steps that you may want to ponder:

1. Practice release.
2. Practice reward.

Practice Release

Earlier in this book, I recounted a very successful family fishing excursion that included the catching and releasing of two beautiful sailfish.

I find it somewhat ironical that today, as I write this very chapter, the boys received in the mail their official Billfish Foundation Release Certificates. The Billfish Foundation, promoting conservation through research, acknowledged the successful release of these grand and proud billfish.

If you desire to modify your behavior, so that out from the Thatch of their past whiffs they are not as apt to discover within you another example of "remembering too well," then practice release.

If you must, catch them in the mistake. Cover it well. Spend some time on it.

That is what these fishermen did. Each listened attentively to the mate's advice. They covered or handled well their tasks. It took each one thirty minutes to land his fish.

Land your point. That is fine. Cover the issue. Cover it thoroughly. Ask questions to verify reception of your instructions. Deal with it then as you think best.

Then release it! Let it go! Just as the Billfish Foundation promotes conservation through research, you will be able to conserve your own energy and the energy of your team members. You will be able to conserve your human resources if you will catch and express your frustration; do it well; then let it go. Practice release!

Practice Reward

Speaking of research, I do know this much. After hundreds of seminars and workshops and consulting sessions, I have learned one fundamental point.

We do not grow when you incessantly and repeatedly point out the fish we lost, the ones who got off the hook, the mistakes we have made. When you repeatedly point out our weaknesses, that is when we self-destruct.

When you mention and release our weaknesses and affirm or reward our strengths, that is when we self-correct. Practice reward!

CHAPTER 7

Performance

The Exasperation

If there is anything that your team members scrutinize, it is your example. It is as if they possess a filtered vision uniquely capable of focusing in toward your example. They will use your example as a justification for their attitude and their behavior.

The reminder formula here is: Expectations minus examples equal exasperations. The perception connection question is: Do they perceive that you expect more than you give?

What Does Expecting More Than You Give Look Like?

In another city, I was the guest at a certain facility. Within the building, there was a small door that obviously led to a special room. Clearly marked on the door were the words: "Dues-Paying Members Only."

If you want to block the door of communication in relationship between you and your team members, then give them the perception that you are not a dues-paying member. Even if you own the place, and thousands of other places like it, you will not be as effective if you give them the impression that you are not willing in any way to example your expectations, to pay the dues yourself. This is true even if you have paid dues for decades in the past. They look for your current example.

Expecting more than you give resembles refusal to pay dues today. Forget yesterday, they are focusing on the dues being paid today. Past experience, past dues paying, even authority, does not in their perception totally absolve one from exampling. Expectations minus examples do equal exasperations. It equals an appearance that indicates you are refusing to pay your dues.

I was in graduate school when I first acutely observed the disparity between expectation and example. One of my professors was a stickler on the issue of being in class on time - as far as the students were concerned. If you were ever late, you were in trouble. Of course, he might not have caught you, because he was always late.

His respect-factor was significantly diminished by his excessive tardiness within an environment that mandated the students' promptness.

Asking more than you are willing to give looks like an incessantly tardy professor mandating promptness on the students' part.

While we are thinking about students, I am reminded of the time when I was giving a presentation in Florida during Spring Break. Spring Break is capitalized because it is a capital-letter experience for many college students. And while I was there, the big thing was to have one's ear pierced.

I did not respond to the invitation to have my ear pierced, but I was intrigued by a particular sign I observed on the beach strand: "Ears Pierced While You Wait."

I wondered then and wonder now if there is any other way to have your ears pierced. How else could it be done? You have to wait!

What Do They See When They See You Coming?

There is ultimately no other way to underscore and enhance your expectations than to example them. Have your work done, not while you watch and wait, but as you example! Example is a verb!!

Granted, this may not be true in every case, but it is a fundamental principle worth noticing: "I do better work when you work. I, at least occasionally, appreciate our mutual participation."

Exampling is much more than tutorial in nature. It is supportive. It looks like company and team and fellowship and cooperation.

When exampling is at least occasionally there, while I work, I am encouraged. If example is never there, or rarely present, while I am working out the expectations, I am exasperated.

Manager, at least periodically, have your work done, not while you watch and wait, but as you example!

How Does One Who Asks More Than He Gives Modify?

If you think it is possible that they occasionally see you as one asking more than you are willing to give, then there are two behavioral modification steps that you may want to ponder:

1. Practice participation.
2. Practice the policy.

Practice Participation

"Swap Shop" is a radio program that I hosted many decades ago. It was basically a public service venture that allowed listeners the opportunity to sell, buy or trade services or products. Now, many years later, I am observing a "swap shop" of a different order.

Many of our large corporate clients are encouraging middle level managers to "swap shop" with each other and with subordinates. This mutual exchange, the on-the-scene and on-hand participation, examples interest, indicates appreciation and opens eyes and ears.

By sampling another's journey, you indicate a desire to pay dues. You secure the feeling similar to the one they have after you multiply the feeling by the decades of their experiences.

By "swap-shopping," you either indicate how it can be done or you learn how it can be done! By "swap-shopping," by practicing participation, you indicate your care, you exhibit your concern.

You example not only expectations of mutuality, you example an interest in the life and work of the one with whom you are swapping. Your participation practice is an antidote to some of their exasperation.

Practice The Policy

It is very difficult to always expect them to be on time if I am incessantly late. It is exceptionally problematical if I always exhort, but never practice, confidentiality. It is downright frustrating if I expect you never to use foul language at work and foul language is all you ever hear me say. It is exasperating if I have a policy of no food in the plant and I visit you while I am eating a hamburger cursed with onion.

If one perceives you as expecting more than you example in the area of performance, then practice the policy - yourself!

If the past whiffs out of their Thatch Huts indicate the raising of their antennae against hypocrisy, then practice participation and practice the policy even if, especially if, they perceive you as the boss!

The Great Gift

In the area of performance, sometimes the grandest and most effective thing you can do is to elicit and receive their performance.

The reminder formula here is: The capacity to receive can equal a great gift. The perception connection question here is: Do they perceive you to be better at giving than receiving?

What Does Being Better At Giving Than Receiving Look Like?

It looks like rejection. It looks like the nonchalant, matter-of-fact, avoidance of a compliment. It looks like the denial of their input, the denial of their participation. It resembles an act that devalues and invalidates them. Now, the importance of this entire Thatch subtype, the area of receiving as opposed to giving as it relates to performance, may catch you by surprise. I must confess that I have wrestled with this issue for many years.

The culture in which I was raised touted the superiority of giving over receiving. Even the One Whom I worship explains it as being more blessed to give.

Nevertheless, my point of wrestling is related to the possibility that occasionally it may be awfully important to receive.

As I tell my seminar participants, I have worked it all out for myself in a certain way. Sometimes the most giving thing I can do is to receive. Many times the grandest gift is reception.

Being better at giving than receiving may look like denial to them. As they look out from the past whiffs of their Thatch Huts, it may look like rejection to them.

It may be as if they are saying, "I am not good enough. You do not need me."

How Do You Modify When You Are Better At Giving Than Receiving?

1. Practice asking.
2. Practice receiving.

Practice Asking

Unfortunately, the number of managers who exhibit concern and compassion for employees and at the same time deny the employees the right to give, to help, to contribute, to co-own ideas, is legion!

Many of you who read this will recognize that your inventory is actually an inventory or stockpile of ideas. Please understand that they want to help birth those ideas. If you want their participation in the journey, let them help draft the map. If you seriously desire their participation on the project, let them help draft the plan.

How Could You Do That So Well?

And, if you really want to catch them by surprise, ask them how they were able to do something so well. You might even want to suggest that, by sharing their ideas with you, they will be helping you. By sharing why they were able to do something so well, they will be teaching you.

What a grand gift for a manager to give another team member - "Would you mind telling me how you did that? I would like to ask you to teach me how to do that."

Practice Receiving

When they give, you receive!

It is better not even to ask, if you are not at least going to listen. This does not mean that you are mandated to buy into and to implement every one of their ideas.

It does mean that in the area of performance we recognize and validate this need to give, to participate, to help birth some of the concepts. Basically, reception does not so much mean implementation as it does attention - listening.

Be careful not to put their ideas on the back burner. Do not put off consideration of what they want to give. Listen while the idea is hot. Do not allow their ideas to evaporate. Be very careful here. You may not only notice the evaporation of their idea, you may notice the elimination of their enthusiasm.

Quite recently, the youngest child scampered into the room. He was clothed in nothing but his shorts. He positioned himself in front of his mom and flexed his muscle. He then yelled, "Look, Mom - quick."

The idea was that he could not hold it long. Constantly reject what they want to give, and they may not be able to hold it long. What was a bulging idea becomes, in their perception, a drooping mistake!

If the past whiffs emanating out of their Thatch Hut reveal a fear of rejection, be very careful. Practice reception - right then! Remember, reception may not always indicate implementation. But it can indicate watching, listening - attention.

CHAPTER 8

Presentation

Familiarization

If Chapter five is by far the longest chapter in the book because it forms the nucleus of our thinking, then this chapter may be one of the briefest chapters because I have just completed an entire book on the subject of presentation. Accordingly, the structure of this chapter may be altered somewhat.

But I do want to address here the reality that how they perceive you, what they see when they see you coming, is certainly related to the manner in which you speak or present in public.

I thoroughly understand that many of you who manage and lead others find many occasions when your presentations in public are mandated. I

What Do They See When They See You Coming?

further recognize that many times the only area in which there is interaction between you and your team members is in the midst of a presentation. Quite possibly, the only time some of them may see you may be when you are speaking in public.

Accordingly, their perception of you will be significantly related to what they see when they see you presenting.

There are two reminder formulae for your consideration here: Style plus substance equals a speech cake! Bones plus meat equals "familiarized" presentations.

The two perception connection questions for your consideration are: Do they perceive you to be prepared? Do they perceive you as a caring and effective presenter?

A detailed examination of subject matter relating to the formula and to the perception connection questions is found in *Celebrate The Butterflies – Presenting With Confidence In Public*. Related bibliographical information can be found in this chapter's note section at the end of the book.

But for now, let me share two observations about presentations and perception:

1. Presentations take time.
2. Presentations mandate preparation.

Presentations Take Time

You might expect that here I would expand on your preparation time. You might suspect that initially I would want to remind you that normally an hour-long presentation necessitates about ten hours of preparation. I will address that later, but I first want to address a larger issue as it relates to perception.

Presentations take time - their time!

Do not ever let it leave your perception that your presentations take their time. Their Thatch may set them up against someone who takes their time for granted!

If you want to tantalize their stinger, then create a situation where it was important enough for them to have to be there to hear your presentation, but it was not important enough for you to be prepared. If you want to slant their perception against you, then tell them to take the time to hear you, but insult them with an unpolished style and material that lacks substance.

If what they see when they see you coming to do a presentation equals nothing more than a hastily thought out and read presentation, then they will perceive you as being unprepared. But, you made or encouraged them to take the time to come and hear you. And, you did not do your part. You did not prepare. Their time appears to be unimportant to you.

If you are unwilling to prepare your presentation, but still encourage them to take their time to hear you, then what leads them to think that you will value them more and prepare more effectively in other settings?

If their time appears unimportant to you while you speak, what should make them think that you value their time in other ways?

If you are not going to prepare your presentation, why should they perceive that you prepare in other areas of work?

It is a matter of the valuing of time - their time. It is a matter of their perception.

Presentations Mandate Preparation

Their perception as it relates to you may have a great deal to do with their perception about your presentations. Their perception about your presentations may largely relate to your preparation.

Preparation exhibited in the writing and the delivery of the speech will influence their perception.

Pay the preparation price in structure and substantive explanation, and they may perceive you as caring about their time. Pay the preparation price to the point that you become familiar with your speech, and they may perceive your effectiveness as moving beyond your presentation into an area that encompasses the whole of your work.

How you speak indicates how you value time - their time! How you speak indicates how well you are prepared.

Supposedly, in their perception, the way you value their time while presenting indicates how you value their time in other circumstances. In their perception, the degree to which you prepare your presentation may equal the degree to which you prepare in all areas of your work. Normally, perfection is not expected here. But they do expect and appreciate your best.

CHAPTER 9

Preoccupations

An Ooziness

ecause you are transparent, much about you leaks out toward them. What they see when they see you coming will be influenced to a great degree by what is going on within and outside you.

If you are bothered by a toothache, the fact that you are uncomfortable may ooze out and cause them to perceive something different from reality. Their perception may differ from your perception. You may perceive that your toothache is driving you crazy. They may perceive your displayed behavior as a displeasure with them.

If you are preoccupied with a friend going through a very difficult time, they may perceive your preoccupation as an indifference toward them.

The reminder formula here is: External and internal events equal ooziness. The perception connection question is: Do they perceive you to be preoccupied?

What Does Preoccupation Look Like?

Preoccupation resembles a mind and a heart and a spirit that are somewhere else. Preoccupation looks like difficulty in focusing. It resembles mind-wandering.

At the best, preoccupation looks like detachment. At the worst, preoccupation appears as rejection. An insecure partner may perceive a preoccupied mind as one that is disinterested, non-caring, cold.

Preoccupation is related to powerful external and internal influences. These inside and outside stimuli may not always be negative in nature.

A manager can be preoccupied with the marathon race she just won, a church project, a fiftieth wedding anniversary party for her parents.

And, a manager can be preoccupied with work.

The Preoccupation With Competence And Compassion

It was a wonderful trip up north. The gentleman who asked me to speak had heard me present overseas and had arranged for me to present a one-day seminar to his staff.

Upon arrival, I would learn that his healthcare facility was focused toward extremely, critically ill patients.

To be on staff was a deliberate and unusually challenging decision. The people who worked there were quite impressive. I was touched by the unique manner in which they were investing themselves into this project. It was as if one by one they were being absorbed into this habitat of caring.

But late in the day, a problem surfaced. Each of us began to notice it. Quite frankly, I was startled, if not embarrassed, that I had not detected it earlier.

Precisely because they were so committed, especially because they were so competent, they were individually slipping into a turf-protective state that was insular in nature. By their own admission, they had become so focused, so immersed into their own tasks and into their individual caring for their patients, that they had become almost callous toward each other. Here, it was not some sort of alien distraction that had them preoccupied. Fueled by their own competence and compassion, they were each traveling their own separate road to the degree that communication was being obliterated.

Their perception of each other was becoming one that indicated a degree of mutual indifference toward each other.

That is what preoccupation, even when it is fueled by competency and compassion, can look like!

Well, they wanted to do something about it. And they did. On that day, they birthed the initial steps toward behavioral modification.

How Does One Modify Excessive Preoccupation?

1. Tolerate it.
2. Turn it around.

Tolerate It

To imagine a state of mind that is totally void of preoccupation is illusion. The goal here is not eradication or elimination of a preoccupied state of mind.

Make it easy on yourself by agreeing with

yourself that it is appropriate to tolerate a certain amount of inner preoccupation. This tolerance positions you for the modification that can be categorized as preoccupation control!

Turn It Around

You begin to control preoccupation's damage by seeking to channel the inclination toward preoccupation in an outward direction.

Seek to become positively and beneficially preoccupied with servicing your team member. By turning it around, by channeling preoccupation toward a positive thrust, you are diminishing the chance of negative, destructive preoccupation.

In reality, we do not exist in a vacuum. The more filled you become with positive preoccupations, the less room for the negative ones.

Certainly, you can take this too far. You can actually become oblivious to reality. Certainly, there will be times when you must be preoccupied with the difficult, the discouraging, the disappointing events within and outside you. But turning preoccupation into a plus, one that is directed toward the servicing of their journey, will help you deal with their possible perception that you are always detached from and disinterested in them.

Seek to become more preoccupied with servicing their journey!

The Bottom

When I was in graduate school, I recall taking a battery of tests. Upon completion of the process, a consultant evaluated the scores.

As he was evaluating one particular test, one that measured the recollection of numbers, he mentioned that I had a perfect score. I asked him what that meant. He responded that it simply meant that numbers were very important to me.

I have traveled my own journey in relationship to that issue, but I suggest the sequence and order of numbers is rather important to your team members.

Where they fall in the order of people and things that you hold together within your head and heart matters to them; where they fall in the numbered scheme of things is very important to them.

The reminder formula here is: A ladder minus a top rung equals the bottom. The perception connection question is: Do they perceive you as one who perceives them at the bottom?

What Does The Bottom Look Like?

It looks like everybody else being more important than this one. It resembles significance being attached to who they are and what they do and insignificance being attached to who this one is and to what this one does. Being on the bottom looks like indifference. When you are on the bottom, you are not important; you do not belong - as much as others belong.

Being on the bottom looks like having no one to watch you play, no one to appreciate your work, no one with whom to share your disappointments and accomplishments.

Busyness breeds a cruel apathy. Busyness births an absorption with oneself and an absorption with super achievers that appears to relegate other team members down to the bottom of the ladder.

Excessive busyness that intentionally or unintentionally puts others down is harmful. Be careful here. Your excessive busyness can blind you to their need to be perceived as one who is more than the bottom rung on your ladder.

How Does One Modify "Bottomizing?"

"Bottomizing" may be a strange and newly-discovered concept. If putting others down is a painful and long-acknowledged tendency, then there are two possible behavioral modifications for your consideration:

1. Pay attention.
2. Attend their function.

Pay Attention

I like to say that paying attention is basically the same thing as fostering retention.

Paying attention equals a five-line note and a ten-minute phone conversation. Paying attention equals questions about them, not incessant statements about yourself.

Paying attention equals a learned skill. It takes time.

Attend Their Function

It will help if you will attend their function. Wear their clothes. Talk their lingo. Attend their function!

Your presence may mean more to them than your presents!

If the past whiffs out from their Thatch Hut indicate an inclination toward being "bottomized," be careful, lest they perceive you as one from the top of the ladder who ignores them.

Pay attention. Attend their function!

CHAPTER 10

Peak Expectations

Never Enough

rowth is cyclical in nature! The cycles come and go. The performance peaks are not automatically larger and higher than the prior ones.

The reminder formula here is: Dipless peaks equal bad curves. The perception connection question is: Do they perceive "it" to be "never enough?"

What Does "Never Enough" Look Like?

Do you want to place a tremendous disadvantage on your people? Then create a situation where they perceive that it must always be better than it has been.

If they perceive "it" to be "never enough," then they actually see the situation as one in which you are never satisfied. They may be indicating that, in their perception, in spite of all they have achieved, you always want more.

When it is never enough, it looks like you are excessively demanding more. Dipless peaks that do not allow for rest and even regression present the subordinate with a plethora of bad curves.

These curves include: disappointment and exhaustion, a feeling of being taken for granted and a feeling of being used, apathy that swells into anger!

How Does One Modify If One Excessively Indicates That "It" Is Never Enough?"

If it is likely that they perceive your excessive and increasing expectations as downers, then there are two behavioral modifications that you might possibly want to pursue:

1. Allow for pauses.
2. Allow for detours.

Allow For Pauses

My observation here is influenced by my perspective as a public speaker and as one who has taught public speaking on the college level for more than a decade.

A pause is a wonderful thing!

Pausing in a presentation provides the speaker with the opportunity to focus, to emphasize, to establish pivotal eye contact, to catch a breath, to bridge from one point to another.

Just as a pause benefits a speaker and his audience, so will a pause, a break, possibly even a dip, benefit the employee and the team.

When you allow for a pausing within your team members, when you allow for the catching of breath, the focusing, the bridging of a gap, you not only indicate that you are a smart and perceptive manager, you indicate as well that you care about the team member.

Allow For Detours

Speaking of caring, you also indicate the degree of your commitment toward the team member when you allow for dips, for detours.

Diplessness is an illusion. In reality, we travel on a dipping road. We produce on a terrain that contains dips. Our performance level will be lowered and raised. To move steadily higher and higher and higher may be exceptionally difficult, if not impossible. Dips happen! Allow them!

If the past whiffs out from their Thatch Hut indicate that their antennae are raised up against the danger of excessively demanding expectations, then ponder how they may be perceiving you.

When they see you coming, do they see one who allows for pauses? When they see you coming, do they see one who allows for dips and detours?

Forget to plug into your management an allowance for pauses and detours, they will self-destruct. Factor in time for pauses and detours, they may just occasionally self-correct!

Too Little

The flip side of perceived excessive expectations is the perception that reveals a constant acceptance of the " as is." If excessive expectations can produce some sort of explosion, then complacency can lead to atrophy!

The reminder formula here is: Complacency equals programs for failure. The perception connection question is: Do they perceive you as expecting "too little?"

What Does Complacency, "Too Little," Look Like?

It looks like atrophy!

Just as the various body parts can wither and shrink, so can your various team members waste away. Complacency can birth the stoppage of growth. Complacency breeds the cessation of progress!

Complacency looks like an incessant innuendo that affirms running in place. Complacency can even resemble the implied awarding of sloppy performance and the acceptance of less than adequate attitude.

Complacency can actually stifle enthusiasm. Complacency can look like cold water thrown into the face of a potentially warm spirit; complacency can appear as icy water splashing up against a conceivably hot idea.

The perception of complacency may justify on the part of the team members the following:

- I can get by with what I am doing now.

- Doing better, doing more, is not necessary.
- They do not even seem to care enough to try and help me improve.
- I could do better if someone would even notice what I do now!

How Does One Who Fosters Complacency Seek To Modify?

If the past whiffs from their hut of Thatch indicate an unusually intense disposition to swallow or reject complacency, and if they may perceive you as fueling their fire or feeding their frozenness, then there are two behavioral modifications that you may want to ponder:

1. Practice gentle squeezes.
2. Turn the bottle upside down.

Practice Gentle Squeezes

I love french fries!

As a matter of fact, I am about to place this pen on the desk, hop in the car, and head to a downtown restaurant with my wife.

Now, this restaurant is known for grand hamburgers and hot, fresh, crisp french fries. I love them.

The Power Of Perception Over Reality

But my french fries must always be blessed with ketchup! Ketchupless french fries do not cut the mustard!

Sometimes, it is very easy for me to pour the ketchup onto the french fries. Other times, my attempts at pouring produce difficulty, if not trauma.

I do not know why ketchup gets stuck to the insides of the bottle so easily!

Basically, there are two types of ketchup bottles - plastic bottles and glass bottles. I seem to have trouble occasionally with both of these containers of ketchup.

But I am beginning to learn how to respond to their reluctance to release ketchup.

When securing ketchup from a plastic bottle is difficult, you gently squeeze the bottle. A strong, tight squeeze will not work. It simply cuts off the entire flow. It calls for a gentle squeeze.

Similarly, if they perceive you as fueling complacency, you may want to call for a gentle squeeze. A tight, strong squeeze will simply cut off the flow of their productivity.

But to be concerned enough to softly address their complacency may be the gentle squeeze that brings forth the ketchup of growth, of moving beyond, of improvement.

Gentle squeezes can come in the form of careful and compassionate criticism.

Granted, it may require a conscious effort here, a drastic behavioral modification on your part. But a gentle squeeze, administered clearly, competently, and with a genuine concern, may start the flow and prompt movement out of complacency.

Turn The Bottle Upside Down

But remember, not all ketchup bottles are plastic and squeezable. Some ketchup bottles are glass and breakable. Be very careful here.

Just as it is sometimes necessary to turn the bottle upside down in order to receive ketchup from the bottle, sometimes it is necessary to turn things upside down in such a way that you catch the attention and the potential of the complacent one.

Here, turning the bottle upside down may look like a very serious dialogue, a shift change, a realignment of needs in relationship to skills, rescheduling and monitoring.

One thing that turning the bottle upside down should not look like is an exaggerated competitiveness inside the team that actually hampers an aggressive participation within the marketplace!

The Power Of Perception Over Reality

If the ketchup will not flow, if complacency will not gradually evaporate through a gentle squeeze, then try turning the bottle upside down.

If they possibly perceive you as affirming complacency, if you refuse to try either the gentle squeeze or the turning of the bottle upside down, then complacency may eventually equal programs for failures. The ketchup may become permanently clogged!

CHAPTER 11

Punishment Syndromes

Getting Even

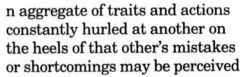n aggregate of traits and actions constantly hurled at another on the heels of that other's mistakes or shortcomings may be perceived as being characteristic of one who is exceptionally focused on getting even!

The reminder formula here is: "I caught you" plus "This is what it will cost you" equals "I quit before I quit." The perception connection question is: Do they perceive you as one always trying to get even?

What Does Getting Even Look Like?

Your actions may be corrective in nature. Your motives may be pure. But when something happens that they do not appreciate, they may perceive you as a villain, the bad guy. Getting even may be perceived as anything you do that they feel inflicts pain or loss on them.

Your getting even may look like a bad shift, your failure to speak, your cronying around with everyone but them. Even excessive teasing can be perceived as torture by them.

You may mean nothing harmful at all. Though we have strongly suggested that this can be said about each of our Thatch-types, it is particularly true here. The way you perceive your action and the way they perceive your intention will not necessarily mirror each other.

In reality, you may not desire to inflict harm on them, yet they may perceive you as always attempting to get even because their Thatch Hut involves the experience of another person who always sought to get even.

Remember, we all carry baggage, and in some cases garbage. Perceived attempts at getting even may be fueled by past experiences.

They may even perceive your getting even as your way of constantly making it so difficult on them that they will decide to quit; it will not become necessary for you to have to fire them.

How Do You Modify Behavior That Exhibits Getting Even?

If their past whiffs from the hut of Thatch indicate an inclination to easily detect efforts at getting even, if you think there may be at least a limited amount of merit to their perception of you in this vein, then there are two behavioral modifications that you may want to ponder:
1. Forego temporary satisfaction.
2. Pursue long-term fulfillment and establish trust.

Forego Temporary Satisfaction

If you now consider it possible that your failure to speak to them may be perceived by them as a getting-even device, then, even if not speaking to them gives you some temporary satisfaction, forego the satisfaction, think in the long term - speak to them.

What Do They See When They See You Coming?

Even if you temporarily enjoy a gathering without them, and think it possible that they may perceive their denial of attendance as your get-even ploy, then invite them. In the long run, you may be better off. If you include some, include all.

Think long and hard before you do something that they perceive as an intentional effort to hurt, or to get them to quit.

A specific behavioral modification here is to think as a caring one, to think in the long term!

Sometimes the urge coming from within is to take out our frustrations on the ones most important and most valuable to us. We do this because we feel less threatened by them. It is as if we are getting even with the situation by taking our frustration out on them. It is as if we are dealing with our own internal state of mind by taking out our frustration on them.

But when they see us coming, they may be perceiving these actions as directly aimed at them, directly indicating our displeasure with them, directly indicating our desire to force them to leave or to quit.

They may be willing to take only so much of our camouflaged frustration. They may be able to tolerate only a limited amount of our external display of an internal chaos. They may become so frustrated that they actually quit before they quit. Their presence, not their performance and productivity, is all you get!

Please do not trade off the temporary satisfaction of somehow making yourself feel better in a way that they perceive as punishment. Do not trade off temporary satisfaction for long-term fulfillment.

Pursue Long-Term Fulfillment And Establish Trust

When you think in the long run, you weigh more carefully your perceived expressions of punishment. When you think in the long run, you certainly become more tolerant. When you think in the long run, you weigh perception carefully. You recall that strengths and weaknesses ride in the same car. Accordingly, appreciation and tolerance become some sort of fellow travelers.

If you think what they may occasionally see when they see you coming is one who is bent on getting even, then ponder the long term.

If they feel frustrated long enough, what will the end result be? If, on the other hand, they feel you have confronted them with a degree of directness and concern, and then dropped it, what will the end result be? Think in the long run!

Embarrassment

The summer of '93 has rediscovered the cowboy movies of the fifties and sixties. Reruns and adaptations are in vogue.

I recall quite vividly growing up with the black hats and the white hats, Tonto and Silver, the Lone Ranger and the Rifleman, Bonanza and Gun Smoke!

Occasionally, a central theme within these various cowboy movies would involve a township rising up to take matters into its own hands.

From their perspective, the law had failed. On their own, the private citizenry would find and seek to punish the villain.

Quite often, the setting for this punishment would be the intentional humiliation of a public hanging.

As we consider humiliation here, the reminder formula is: Your display of displeasure may equal their humiliation. The perception connection question is: Do they perceive you as seeking to punish them through embarrassment?

What Does Embarrassment Look Like?

It can look like a public humiliation. It can look as if you are trying to put them down in public.

Again, in their perception, even excessive teasing may look like torture to them. Public criticism, even if it looks like exaggerated teasing, can appear as embarrassment to them. Careful confrontation must take place in private - or at least with only one or two other participants for verification purposes and for purpose of record.

There will certainly be occasions when one or two other people have to be in the room with you. The one being confronted may even understand and appreciate the presence of one or two other people. However, that one will certainly not understand and appreciate your public criticism.

How Does One Modify Embarrassment?

As criticism is the pivotal issue of embarrassment here, it will be helpful to ponder two possible behavioral modifications:

1. Eliminate intentional embarrassment.
2. Choose verifiers carefully.

Eliminate Intentional Embarrassment

Embarrassment will happen unintentionally. I was informed by a friend that I embarrassed him every time I mispronounced his name. I had intentionally altered the pronunciation of his name and created what I thought was a very clever nickname. For years, I had not thought that he minded. I actually thought he appreciated it and found it funny. He did not appreciate it. But I certainly did not intentionally seek to embarrass him. However, in this case, unintentional embarrassment did take place. Unintentional embarrassment will happen!

Intentional embarrassment does not have to happen. Your display of your displeasure does not have to equal their public humiliation.

You may not even mean for it to equal humiliation; you may not even conceive that it would equal humiliation. Embarrassment, like other management-related issues, has much to do with their point of view.

Practice the elimination of intentional embarrassment!

Choose Verifiers Carefully

I well recognize the need for someone else to be in the room in many situations of criticism or confrontation. I refer to these people as "verifiers". I understand that the verifier, the third party to the corrective or confrontational session, may be extremely necessary.

Choose your verifiers carefully. Choose ones who value confidentiality. Do not intentionally choose the very ones that would aggravate and fuel embarrassment for the interviewee, the evaluatee, the one you are criticizing.

If out from their Thatch Hut, they recall past whiffs of others who embarrassed them, they will likely scrutinize you at this point! Eliminate intentional public humiliation and embarrassment. Do not intentionally embarrass them. Choose verifiers carefully.

CHAPTER 12

Praise

Affirming

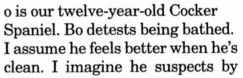

Bo is our twelve-year-old Cocker Spaniel. Bo detests being bathed. I assume he feels better when he's clean. I imagine he suspects by now that a thorough washing is even good for him. Nevertheless, Bo possesses an aversion against his bath and incessantly tries to wiggle himself out of it.

Similarly, many of us seem to exhibit an opposition toward praising others. It is as if we are reluctant to affirm others.

I suppose we know we would feel better after we did it. I further suspect that we recognize that affirmation is good for us, good for them, good for the team. But nevertheless, many of us seek to wiggle our way out of affirming others.

What Do They See When They See You Coming?

The reminder formula here is: Confrontations minus affirmations equal discouragements! The perception connection question is: Do they perceive you inept at affirming?

What Does Affirming Look Like?

Affirming looks like a cleansing. It washes away doubt and replaces their ambiguity about your feeling toward them and their performance with the pleasurable and certain fragrance of acceptance.

If affirmation is so good for us and them and the team, then why do we wiggle so against it? Why do we try to wiggle our way out of it? What explains the aversion that many of us have to affirmation?

We resist affirming another for reasons that may include the following:

1. Our ineptness with perceiving their need for affirmation,

2. Our inclination that affirmation weakens the one who is affirming another,

3. Our inadequacy with verbalization.

Accordingly, if we want to modify behavior, we need to consider steps related to a possible ineptness, inclination and inadequacy on our part.

How Does One Modify Behavior And Enhance Affirmation Skills?

1. Replace ineptness with skill.
2. Reconsider your inclination.
3. Re-evaluate your adequacy.

Replace Ineptness With Skill

If what they see when they see you coming is one who is cool toward affirmation, reluctant toward praise, then their perception may be justified or explained by your feeling that your opinion is not important to them. Part of the problem may simply be that you do not understand how important you are to them. You do not comprehend how much they need you and your affirmation.

You may be assuming that they know how you feel. They do not automatically know and may never know how you feel until you recognize that their knowing how you feel about them is important to them. Only confront another, never affirm that other, that one will become discouraged.

Do not just think affirming thoughts about them. Affirm them!

You can develop a skill that will detect time and again the need for your affirmation. It will be as if your inner antennae are automatically raised to assist you in detecting another's need for affirmation.

Start looking for it. Start looking for their expressed need for affirmation. You will find it. You will see it. You will develop the skill to perceive it.

Reconsider Your Inclination

An aversion to affirmation may not be skill-related. An aversion to affirmation may actually be related more toward one's own inclination of perception.

There is something within many of us that raises internal red flags when we start to praise another. It is as if we are saying, "Wait a minute. What am I getting ready to do here? If I praise her, what does that do to me?"

And the implication quite often is that my praising of another somehow diminishes me. It is as if one is saying, "If I build you up too much, I hurt myself."

All of this actually implies that there is some sort of bank account of affirmation. If I spend it on you, there is less for me or you or anyone else to spend on me.

This does not make sense. But it is reality-based thinking in the eyes of many. They defend their thinking with, "There is only so much to go around."

To the contrary, there is an endless inventory in this bank account. Really, when you take affirmation out of the account and share it with another, you actually increase the affirmation account. The more you give, the more there is to give.

Giving affirmation does not diminish you; it enhances you. Giving affirmation positions you into the process of becoming a more caring and competent manager.

Re-evaluate Your Adequacy

Your aversion to affirming may have nothing to do with ineptness as it relates to the need to perceive their need for affirmation. You may well recognize that need.

Your aversion to affirming them may have nothing to do with the presence of an inclination that holds to the opinion that affirmation diminishes rather than enhances the one who affirms another. You may well recognize the fulfilling and mutually beneficial function of affirmation.

Your aversion to affirming may, however, be related to a perceived inadequacy on your part about your capacity to verbalize your feelings of affirmation toward another.

Perhaps you are uncomfortable about praising another. Your uneasiness may be related to the fact that you think you will sound phony. Perhaps you feel that your motives will be questioned. Maybe you do not know how to word it all. You may not know how they will react.

All of your feelings may be very valid. I can say only that they probably are much more interested in your willingness to affirm than they are concerned about your cleverness. They are probably much more interested in the fact that you take time to affirm rather than how well you verbalize your affirmation.

Adequacy as it relates to verbalization is largely influenced by your willingness to say something affirming. Adequacy here is also largely determined by your sincerity.

Practice a willingness in the area of affirmation. Exhibit sincerity. Take the first two steps of willingness and sincerity; the rest may follow. Adequacy may eventually swallow up inadequacy.

You may have noticed that this Thatch-type is not broken down into subtypes. That in no way should diminish its significance. Here, a standing alone as an entire Thatch-type indicates the simplicity and stoutness of this issue.

If out from their Thatch Hut they have experienced little praise, then catch them by surprise!

Part Three

The Trail &A Tale

CHAPTER 13

The Trail of Modification

hortly after our Delta jet left Salt Lake City, the passenger seated beside me pointed outside the window and exclaimed, "Would you look at that!"

"That" was what appeared to be several Navy jets - the Blue Angels.

I have never seen them before. But on this day, even from a distance, I was enthralled with their proximity to each other and with the mechanical precision of their synchronized movement. It was beautiful. I wish it had lasted longer.

What did last longer was the condensation trails they left behind!

What Do They See When They See You Coming?

This book is about to end. Presumably, you will soon finish its pages. These pages may even soon fly off in the direction of another reader. But I do hope some condensation trails will remain behind for you!

Please do allow this to linger behind and within you - your ability to lead them has everything in the world to do with how they perceive you and with how you modify your management. How they perceive you is your business!

Please allow this to trail behind and within you - effective management and possible management modification equals your attitude plus your behavior plus your perception.

Please allow this to dangle behind and within you wherever you go - your perception is not automatically and merely a template for their perception. Management modification mandates that you perceive this. They may not perceive you the same way you perceive yourself. Their "I remember when" may differ from your "I do not remember saying that."

Please let this follow behind and within you - they do not so much resemble cowboys who wear guns in holsters as much as they resemble people who live in Thatch Huts and wear magnifiers and minimizers. Their perception leads them toward a tendency to distort, enhance, magnify and minimize what you say and what you do. The management modifiers that we have discussed in this book will help equip you for a response to their distortion.

Whereas the condensation trails of the Blue Angels eventually fade away, the trail of modification does not have to evaporate. Instead of diminishing, the management modification trail can actually increase as you learn to sculpt your skills in this area.

As you get ready to travel on, please do not get off this trail - the trail of management modification. Do not lose your way. Stay on the trail!

The trial of management modification has everything to do with the comprehension of, the clarification of, and the response to A Tale of Thatch!

CHAPTER 14

A Tale Of Thatch

Have you ever pondered those words affixed to the mirrors that are attached to the passenger's door on the vehicle? They simply say, "Objects in mirror are closer than they appear."

By now, it should be obvious that the power of their Thatch is much more closely related to the reality of their perception than it appears.

It is not as simple as it seems. It is not as it appears. Attitude and behavior are important building blocks for relationships. But they are not the only ingredients necessary in constructing patterns of meaningful interaction, communication and effective performance. It may appear that nothing beyond attitude and behavior is involved. But perception can either lead to the way of understanding or perception can get in the way of understanding.

The power of perception is much more than it appears to be. Perception informs impression and can even transcend reality. Perception swallows up external and internal influences and can actually impede or positively influence growth in relationships.

The essence of this book has been an invitation into introspection. Hopefully, it not only has helped you discover the powerful nature of perception; hopefully, it has also encouraged you to ask a question - "What do they see when they see me coming?" The answers that you receive to that question may mandate behavioral modification. This book has suggested steps you might want to ponder.

But, before we close there are two more things I would like to share. Both are personal. One is an observation I want to share; the other is a poem I have written.

The first matter, this point of observation, is an issue that surfaces every time I speak and every time I write. How can I be faithful to all that I am and to the One Who has blessed me with every good gift and not be offensive?

Over the decades, with His help, it has worked out. Accordingly, I cannot end this work without at least stating that it is my experience that our Heavenly Father through Jesus Christ is the ultimate One Who can help us modify behavior.

Having said that, let me thank you for reading this book. Before we leave each other, I hope you will enjoy and benefit from "A Tale of Thatch."

A Tale of Thatch

I am a Tale of Thatch.
In my heart, I wear a patch.
If you wonder what it's like to be like me,
You must first consider what I see.

What I see depends on what I've seen.
Where I am relates to where I've been.
My past hurt is still my major thrust.
My patch holds firm until I trust.

Please come visit my Thatch Hut.
I do not wish that we stay in a rut.
Perhaps - if you discover what I see,
Then together we can be all we are meant to be.

Stephen M. Gower
Summer of 1993

Notes

Chapter Four
The information on night-vision goggles was found in *Time-Life Books, Commando Operation - The New Face Of War*. Alexandria: Time-Life Books, 1991, pp. 119-121.

Chapter five
Helpful reading as it relates to the tendency to excel in weakness confrontation and be inadequate in strength affirmation can be found in Stephen M. Gower, *The Art Of Killing Kudzu - Management By Encouragement*. Toccoa: Lectern Publishing, 1991.

Chapter Eight
Helpful reading in this area can be found in several of the books listed in the Recommended Reading section: Bert Decker, *You've Got To Be Believed To Be Heard*. New York; St. Martin's Press, 1992; Stephen M. Gower, *Celebrate The Butterflies - Presenting With Confidence In Public*. Toccoa: Lectern Publishing, 1993; David Peoples, *Presentations Plus*. New York: John Wiley And Sons, 1988.

Chapter Twelve

Helpful reading in the area of thought and behavior is found in Paul Hersey, *The Situational Leader*, New York: Warner Communications, 1984

Recommended Reading

Bodenburg, Dorothy A. Overachieving Parents - Underachieving Children. Los Angeles: Lowell House, 1992.

Decker, Bert. You've Got To Be Believed To Be Heard. New York: St. Martin's Press, 1992.

Gower, Stephen M. The Art of Killing Kudzu - Management By Encouragement. Toccoa: Lectern Publishing, 1991.

Gower, Stephen M. Celebrate The Butterflies - Presenting With Confidence In Public. Toccoa: Lectern Publishing, 1993

Hersey, Paul Dr. The Situational Leader. New York: Warner Communications, 1984.

Missildine, W. Hugh. Your Inner Child Of The Past. New York: Simon And Schuster, 1963.

Peck, M. Scott. The Road Less Travelled. New York: Simon And Schuster, 1972.

Peoples, David. Presentations Plus. New York: John Wiley And Sons, 1988.

About The Author

Stephen M. Gower is considered one of the country's most powerful speakers. Mr. Gower is nationally and internationally recognized as a specialist in management by encouragement and in the development of communication skills for leadership! His power-packed keynote speeches and seminars have impacted thousands of people across the United States and overseas.

Mr. Gower holds a bachelor's degree from Mercer University and a master's degree from Emory University. He is a member of the National Speakers Association and has taught public speaking on the college level for more than a decade. As founding president of the Gower Group, Inc., and as author, consultant and keynote speaker, Stephen Gower has created a unique approach to human resource development.

Stephen M. Gower's first book, *The Art of Killing Kudzu – Management By Encouragement*, has helped establish him as a national leader in his field. *Celebrate The Butterflies – Presenting With Confidence In Public*, Mr. Gower's second book, reveals a fresh solution on redirecting your nervous energy to work for you as you speak in

What Do They See When They See You Coming?

public. *What Do They See When They See You Coming?* is Mr. Gower's third book.

Other works by Mr. Gower include; *Like A Pelican In The Desert – Leadership Redefined: Beyond Awkwardness, The Focus-Crisis – Nurturing Focus Within A Culture of Change, Upsize Selling – Increase Your Sales With The Mix Of Six and Have You Encouraged Someone Today? – 366 Ways To Practice Encouragement.*

Mr. Gower possesses a rare blend of substance, humor and intensity that will excite and energize any audience. Throughout the country, many national and state associations and Fortune 500 companies have invited him to speak. It is not unusual for the same association, corporation, or community to invite him back repeatedly!

The Gower Group, Inc.
P. O. Box 714
Toccoa, Georgia 30577
1-800-242-7404

What Do They See
When They See You Coming?

The Power Of Perception Over Reality

Also By Stephen M. Gower, CSP

Think Like A Giraffe
A Reach For The Sky Guide
In Creativity And Maximum Performance

The Art Of Killing Kudzu
Management By Encouragement

Celebrate The Butterflies
Presenting With Confidence In Public

Upsize Selling
Increase Your Sales With The Mix Of Six

The Focus Crisis
Nurturing Focus Within A Culture Of Change

Like A Pelican In The Desert
Leadership Redefined: Beyond Awkwardness

Have You Encouraged Someone Today?
366 Ways To Practice Encouragement